Merry

CHRISTMAS

This Books Belongs To

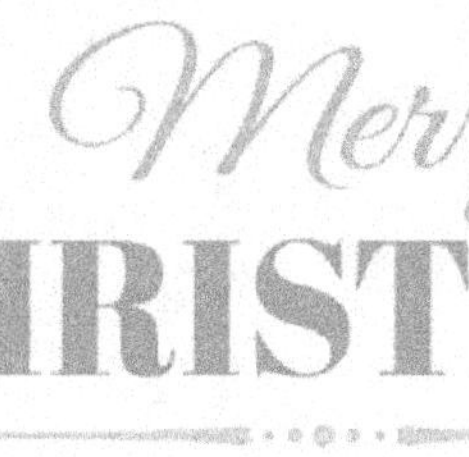

....

....

....

....

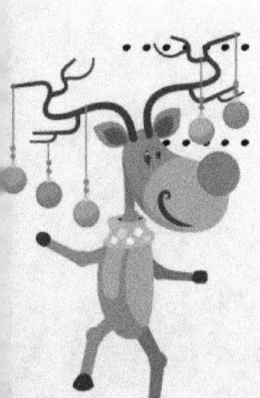
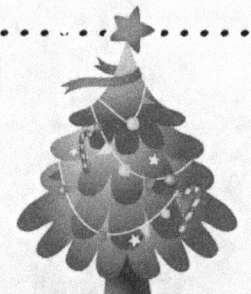
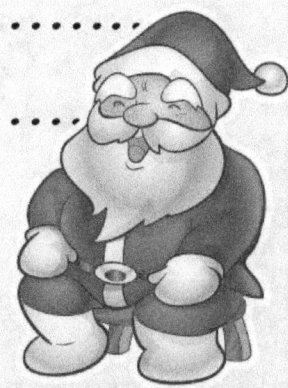

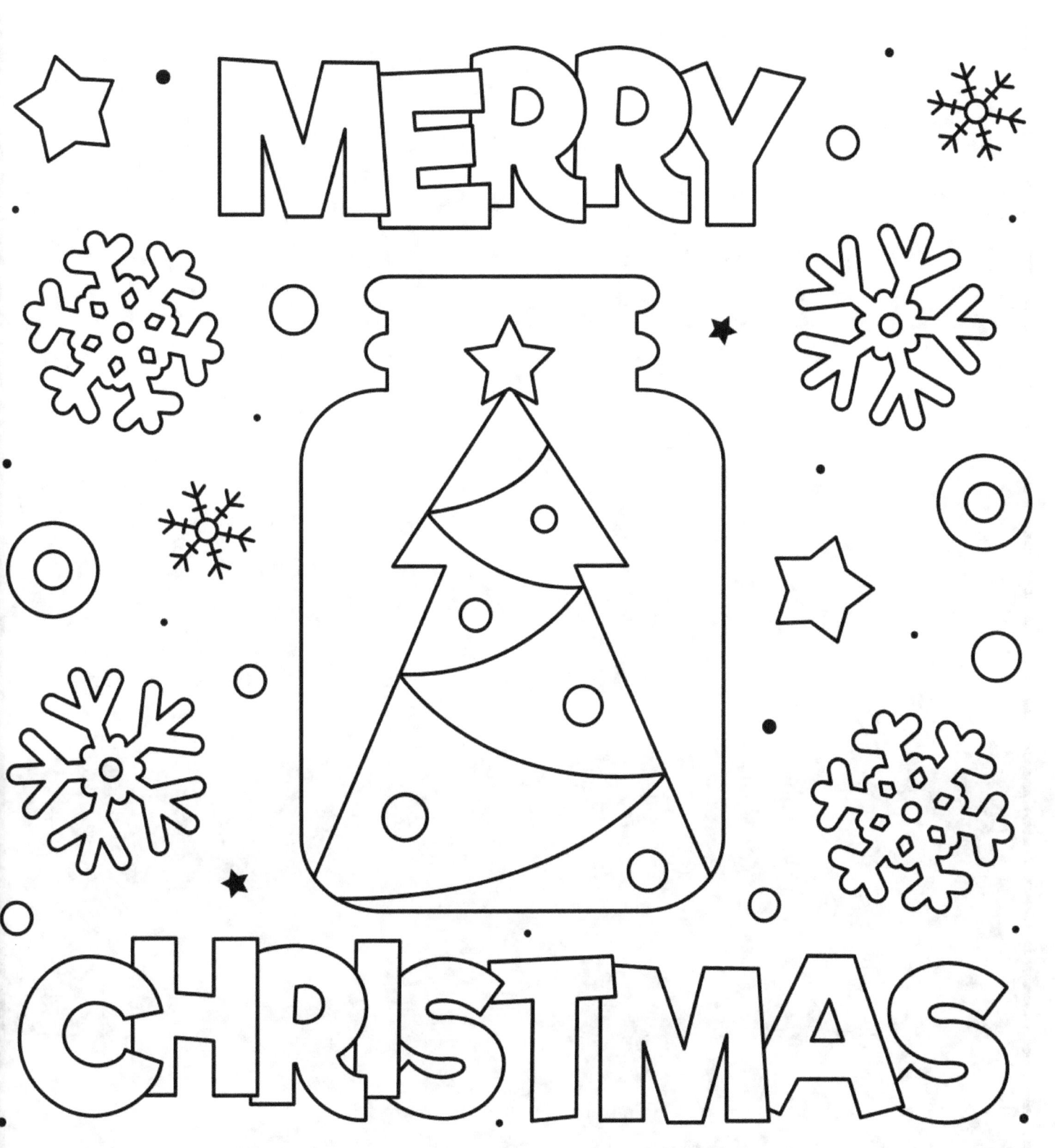

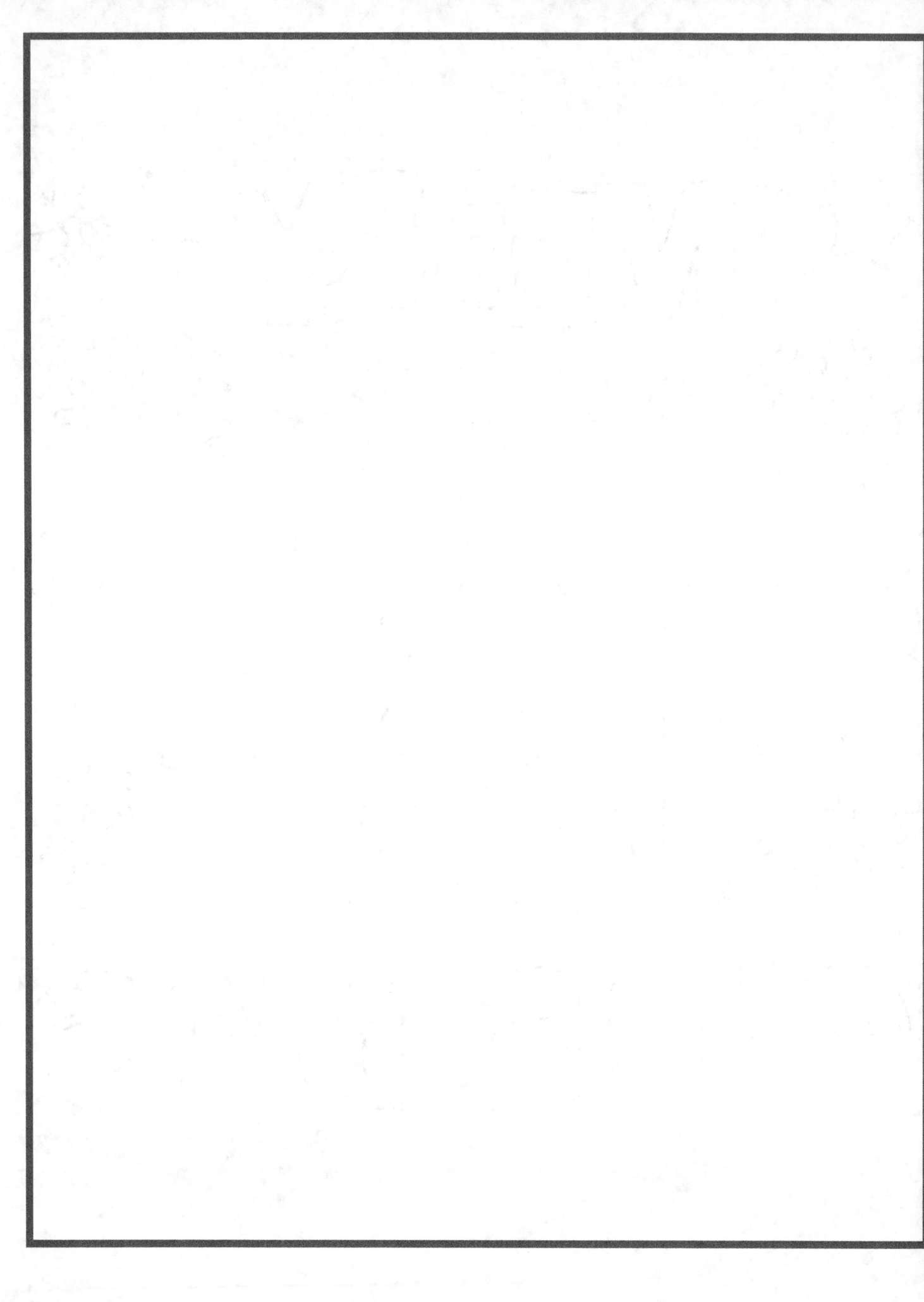

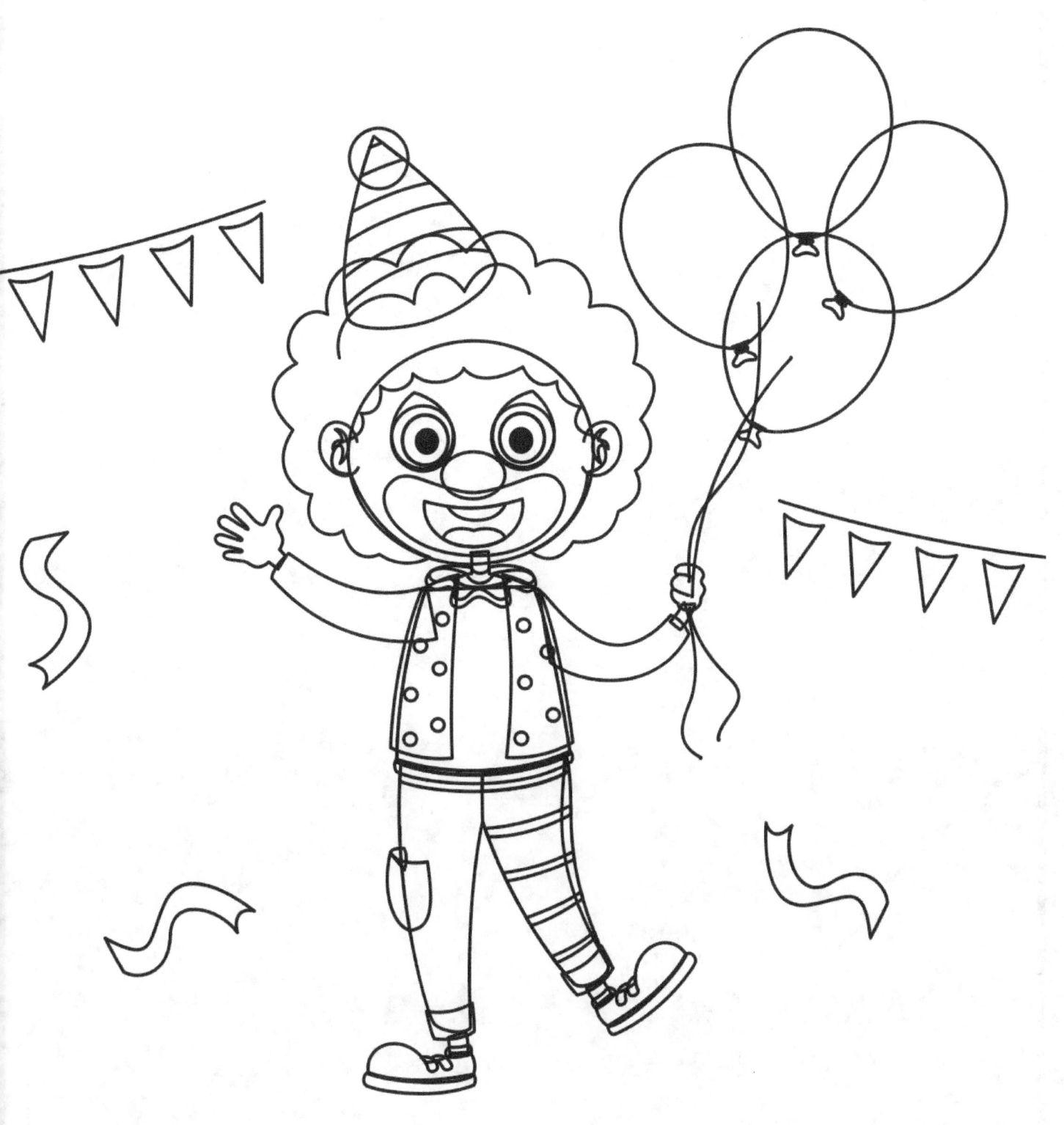

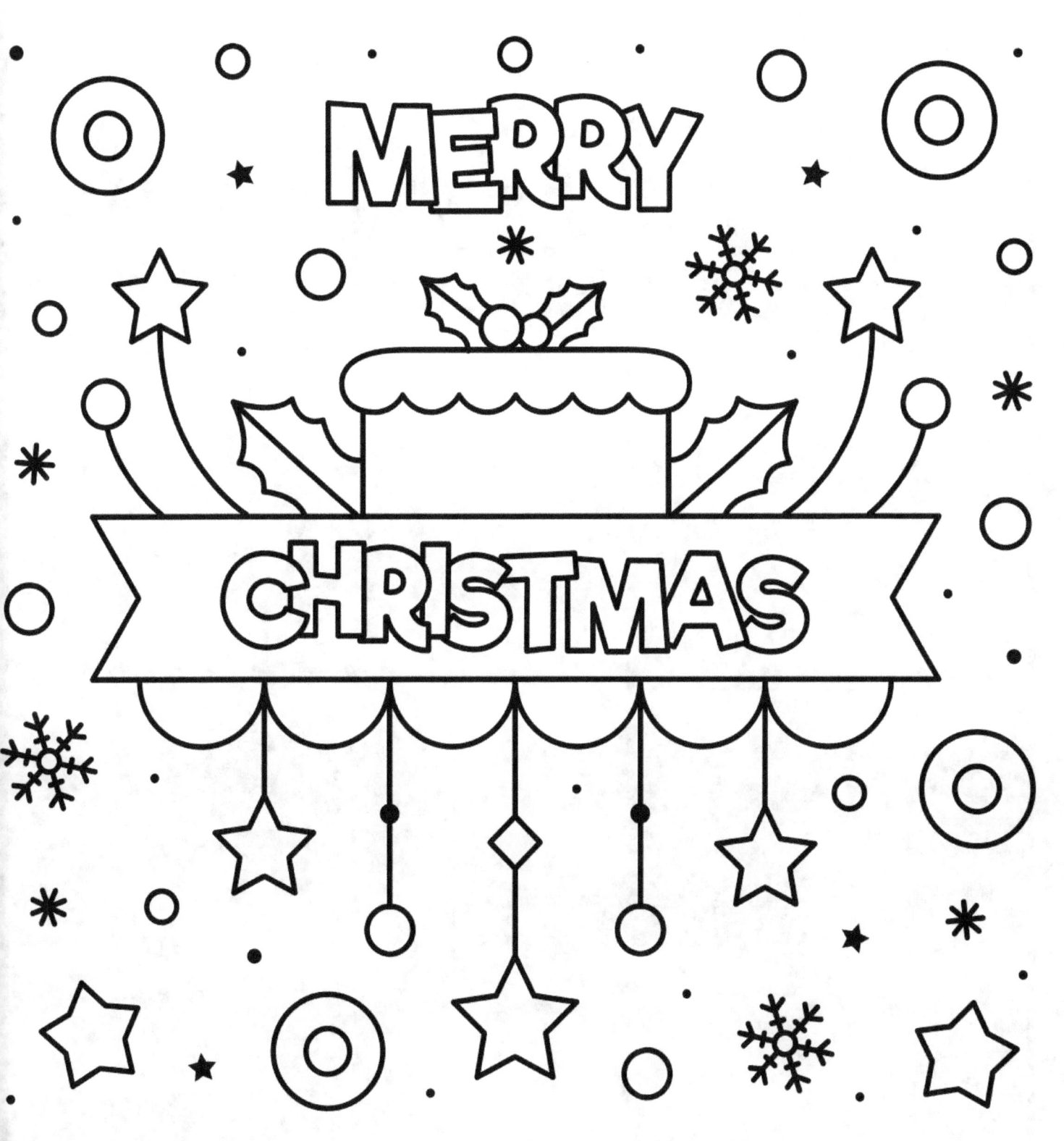

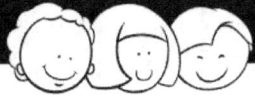

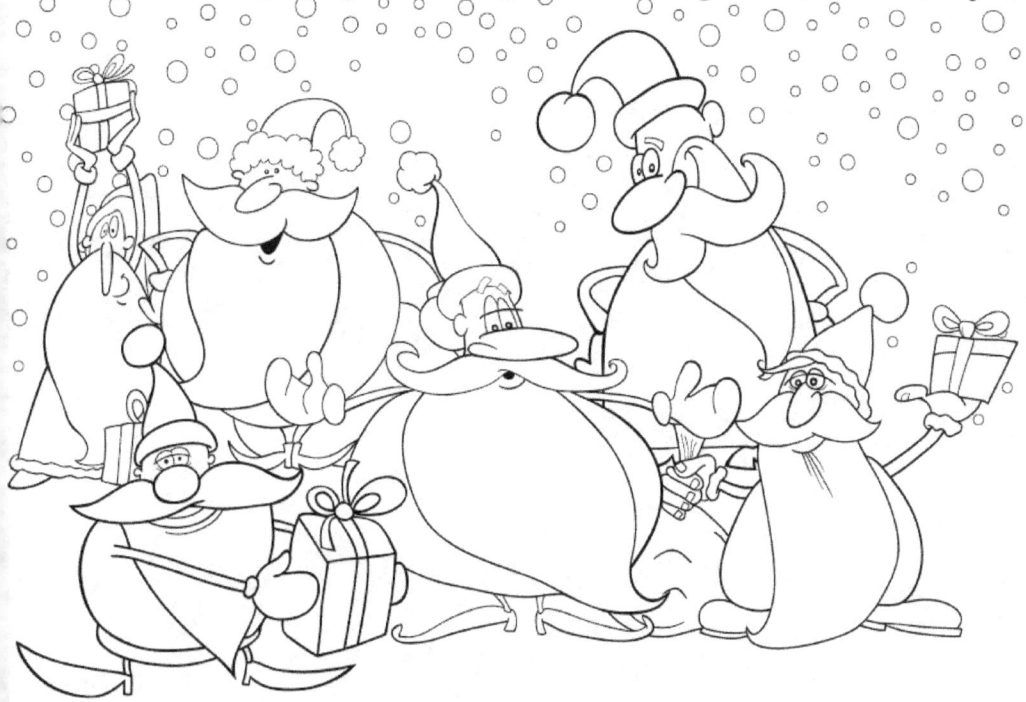

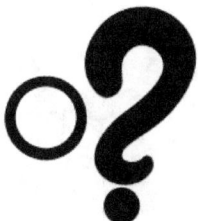

FIND
7
DIFFERENCES

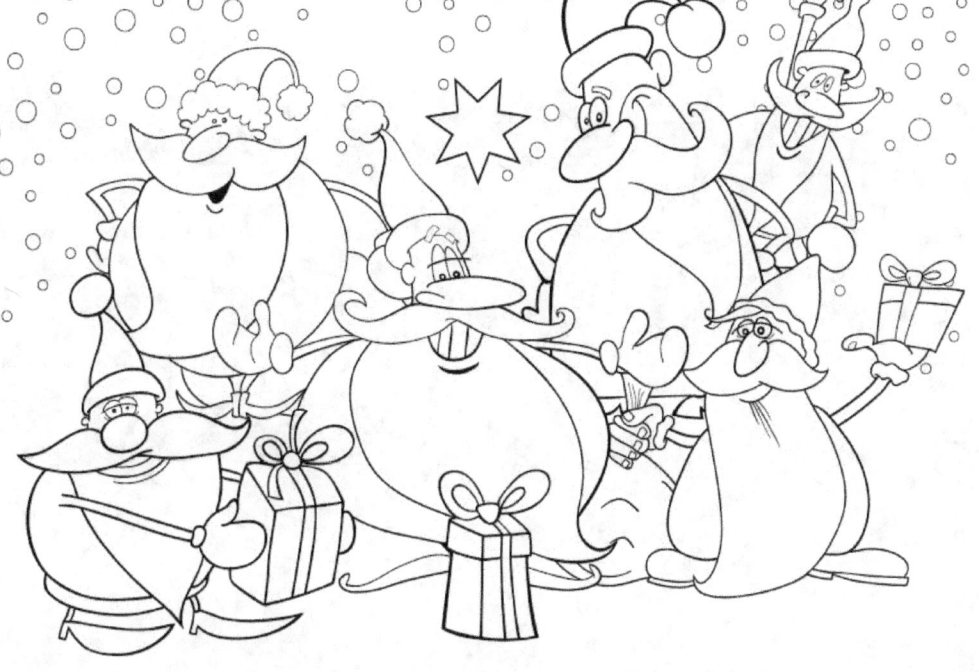

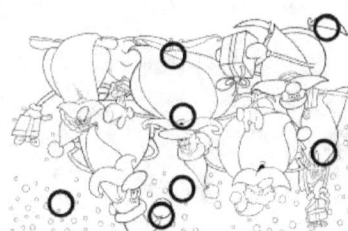

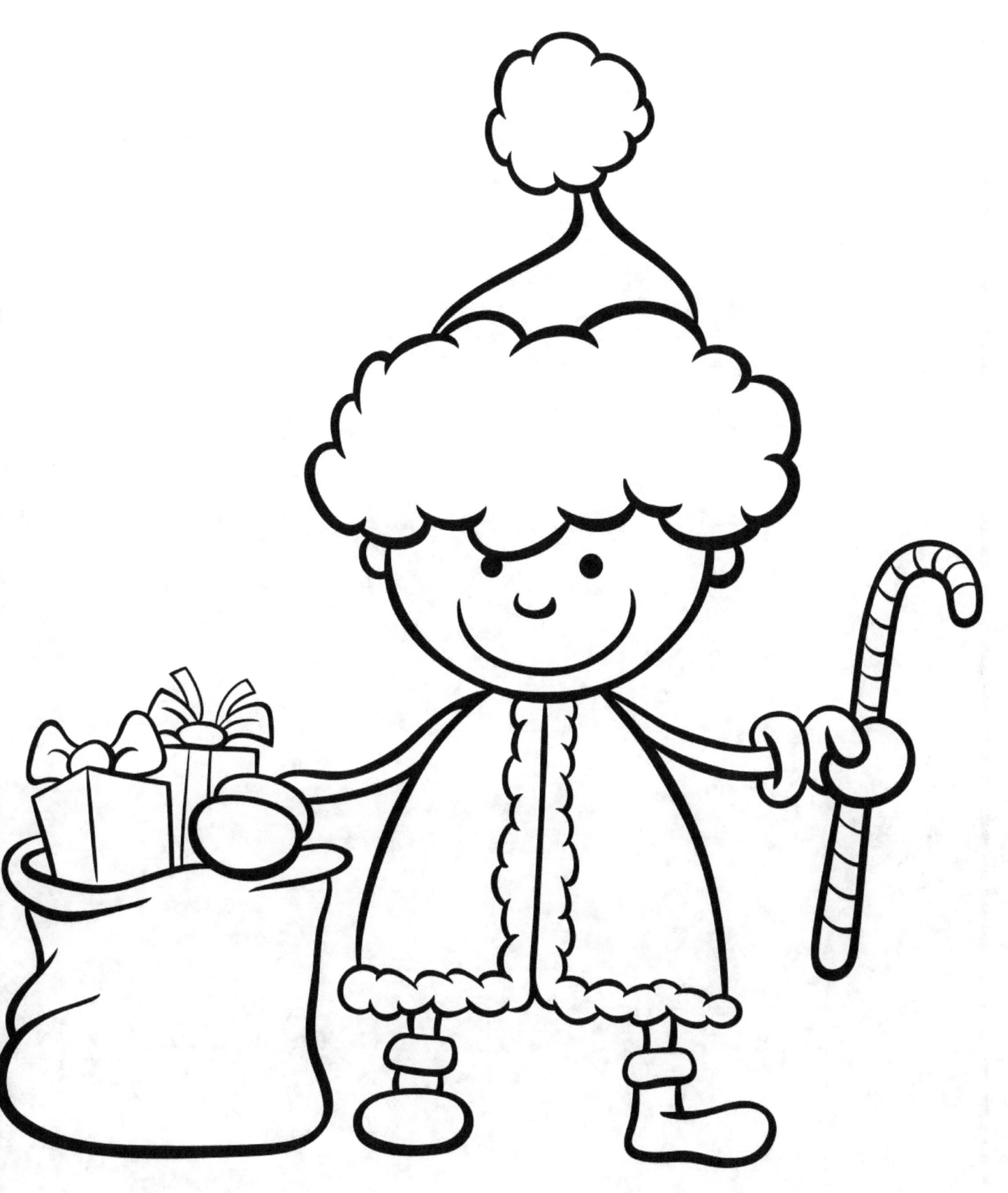

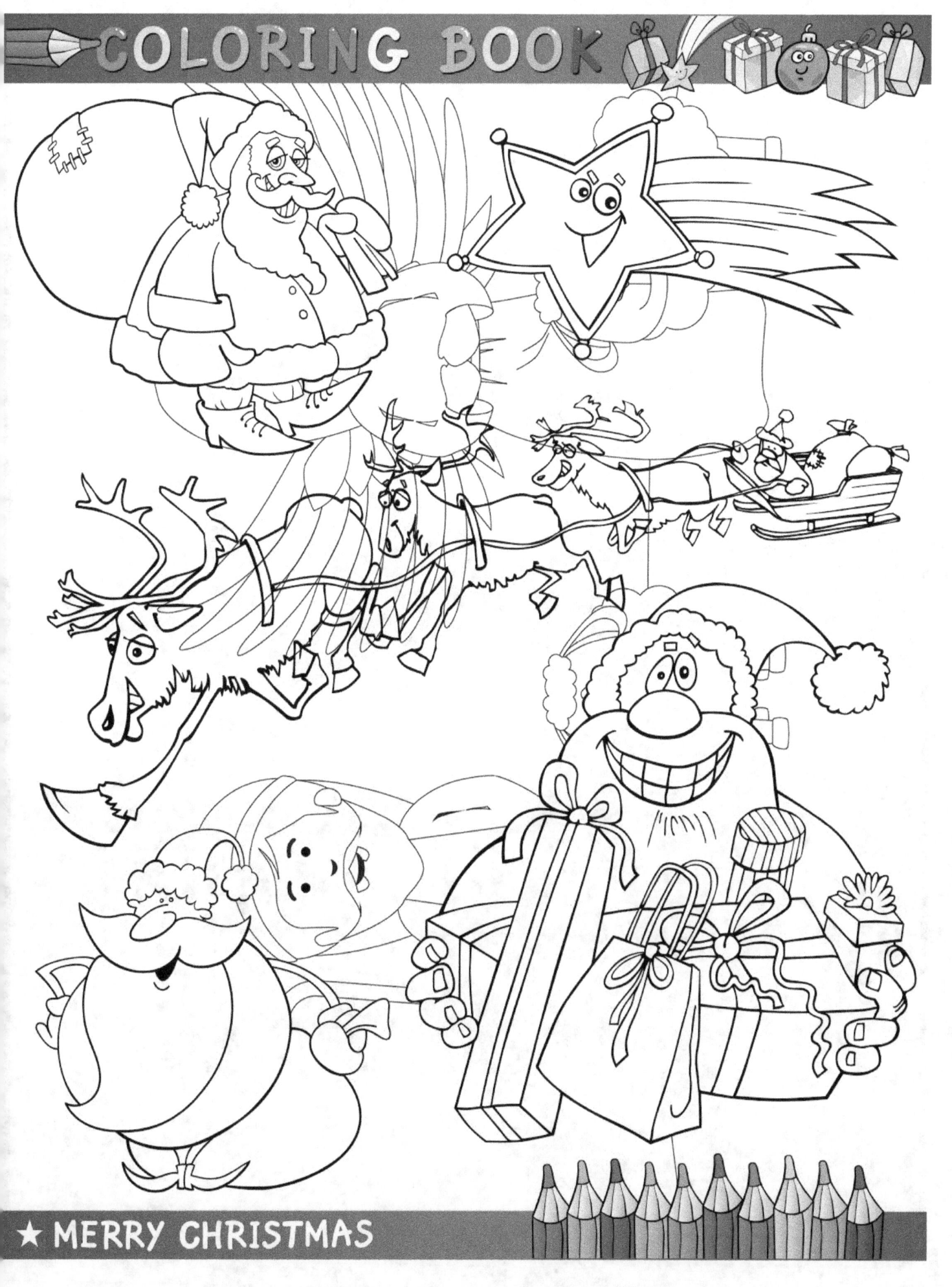

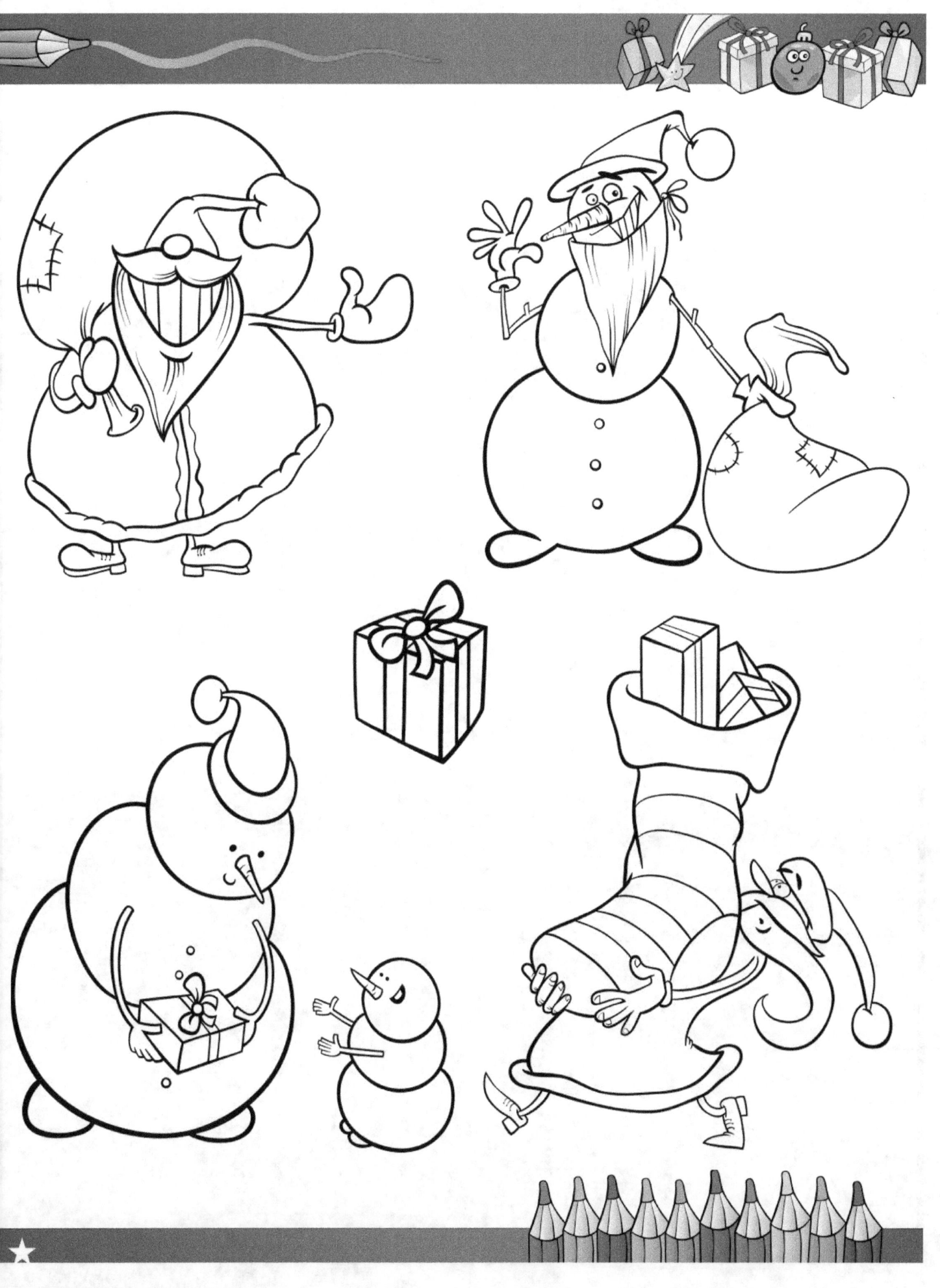

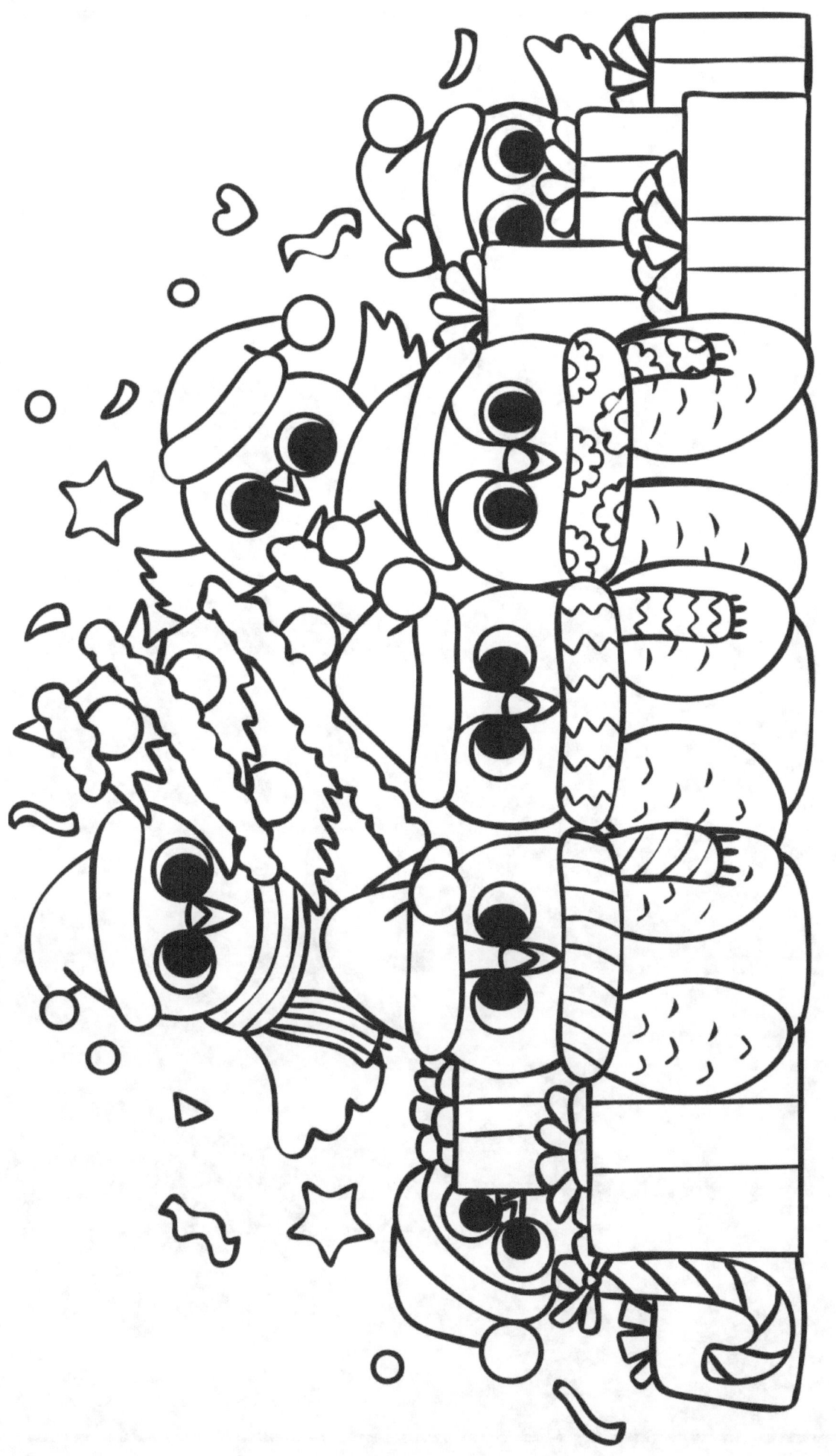

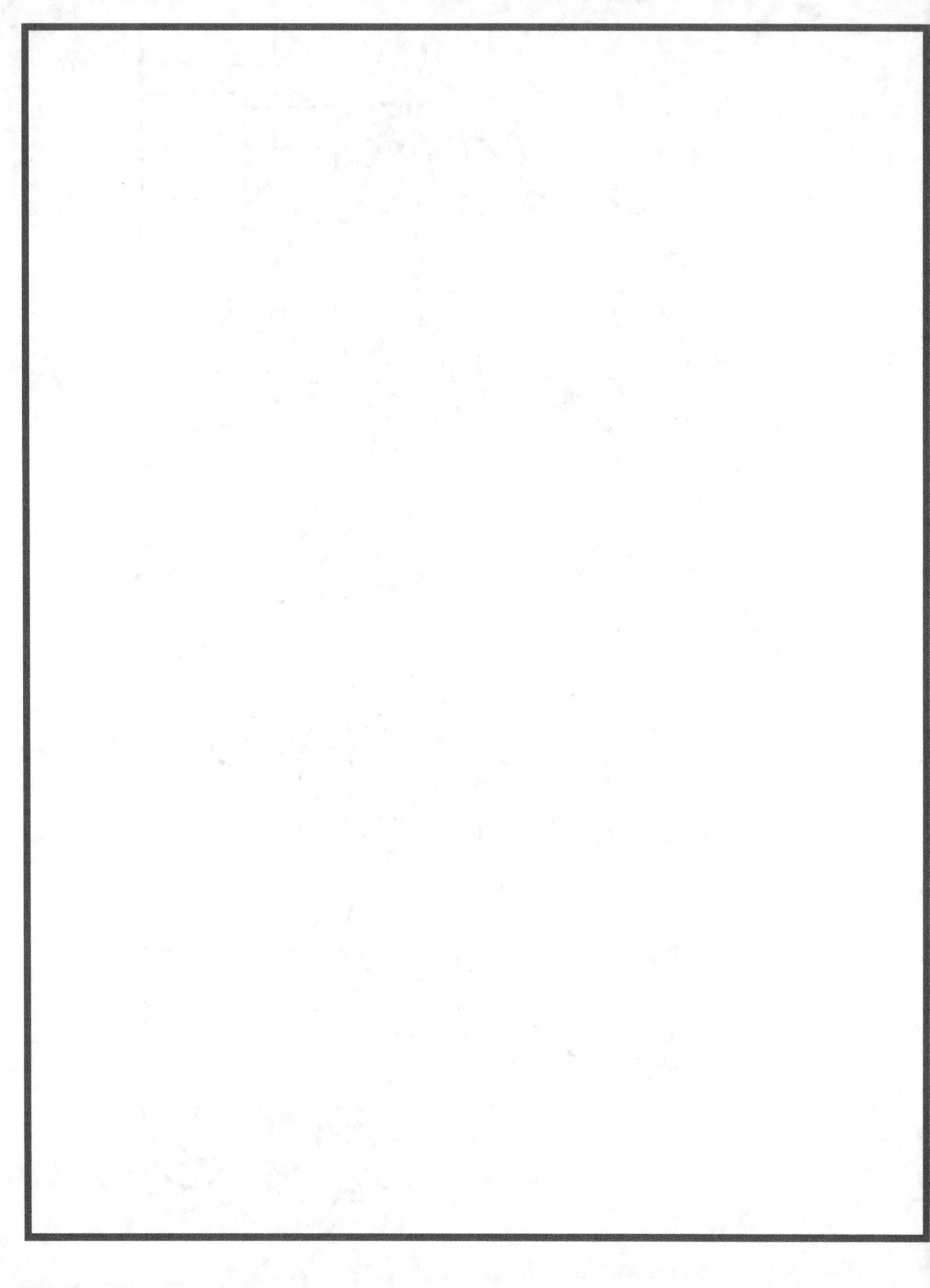

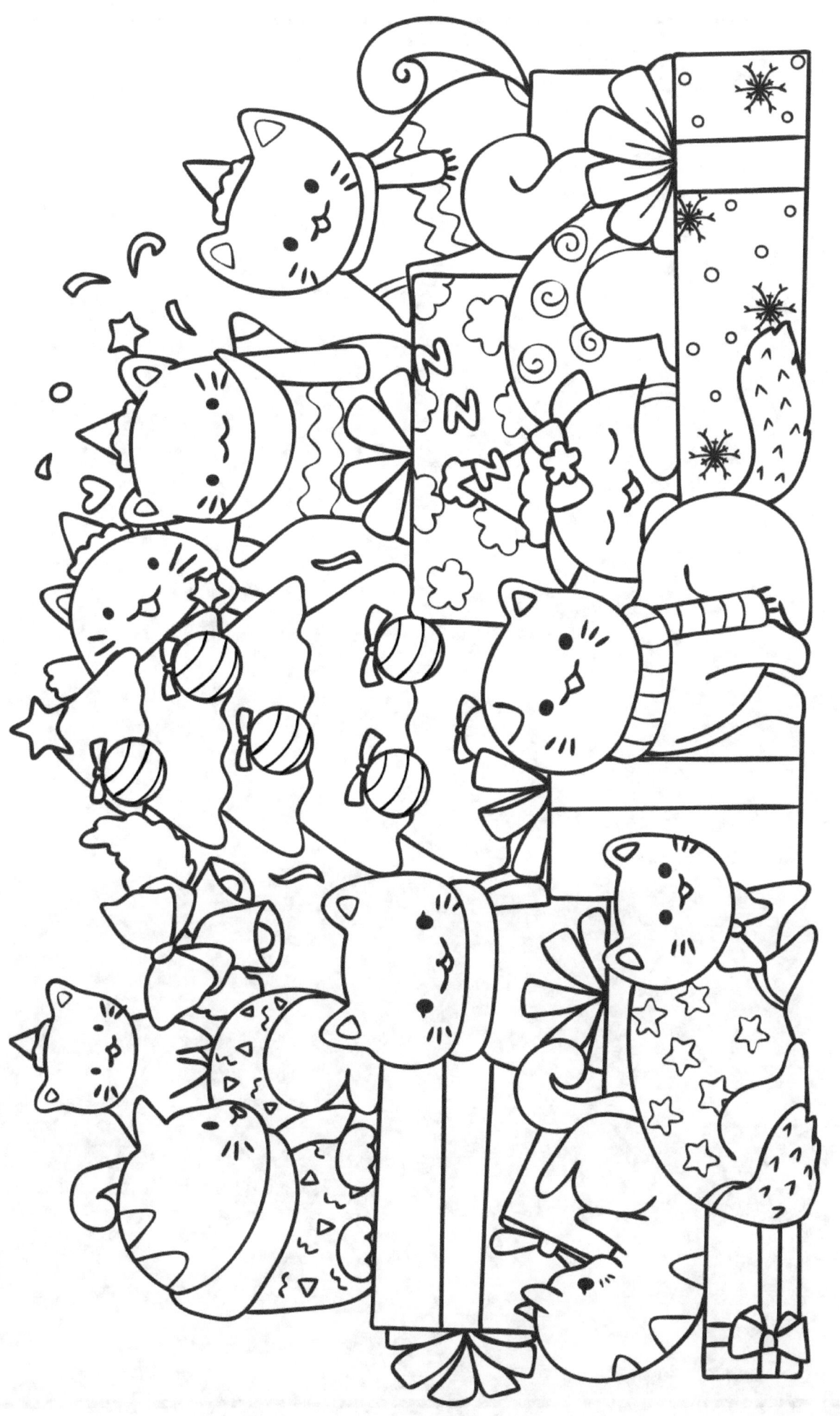

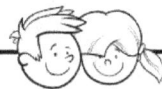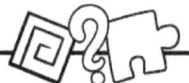

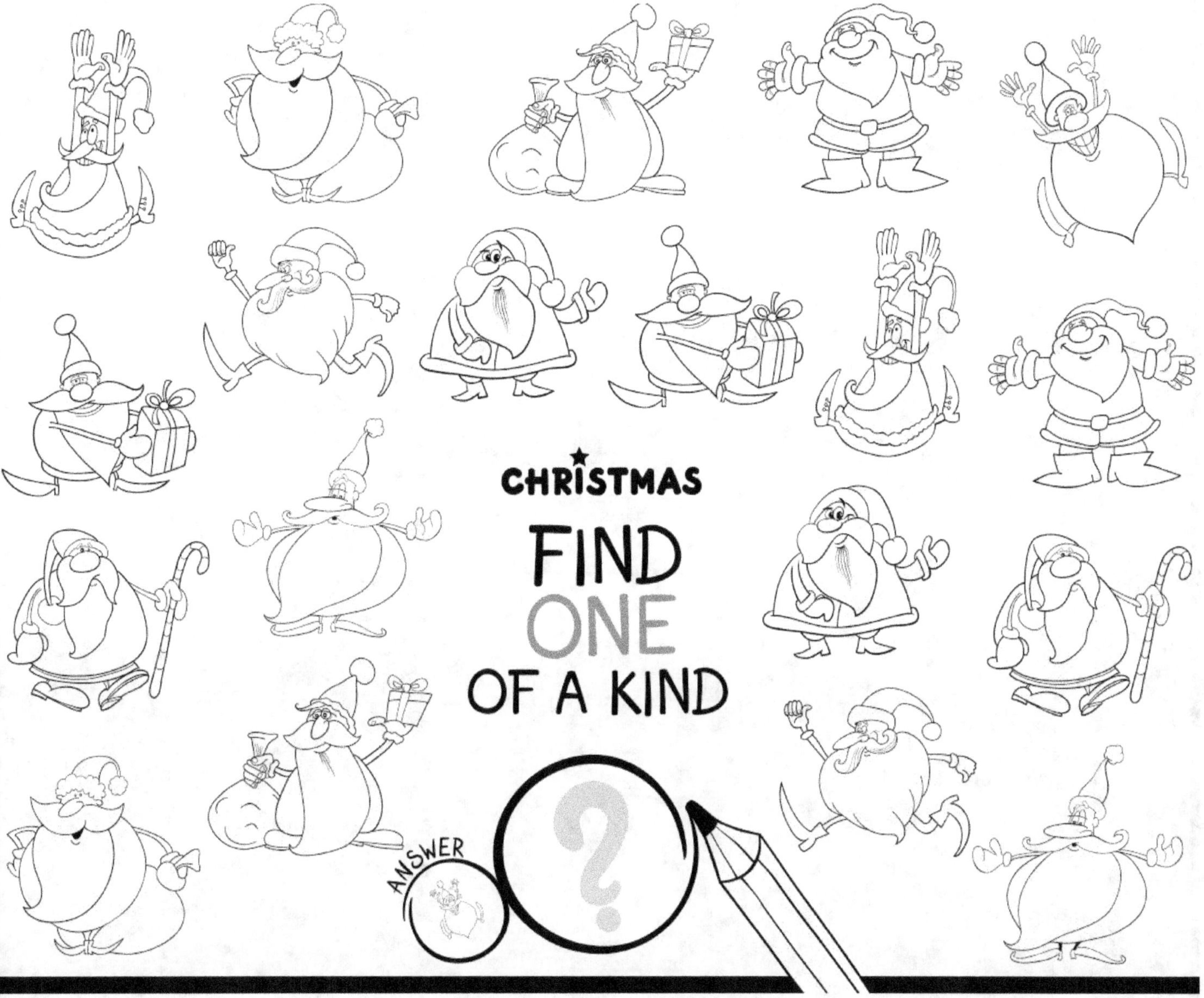

CHRISTMAS
FIND
ONE
OF A KIND

ANSWER

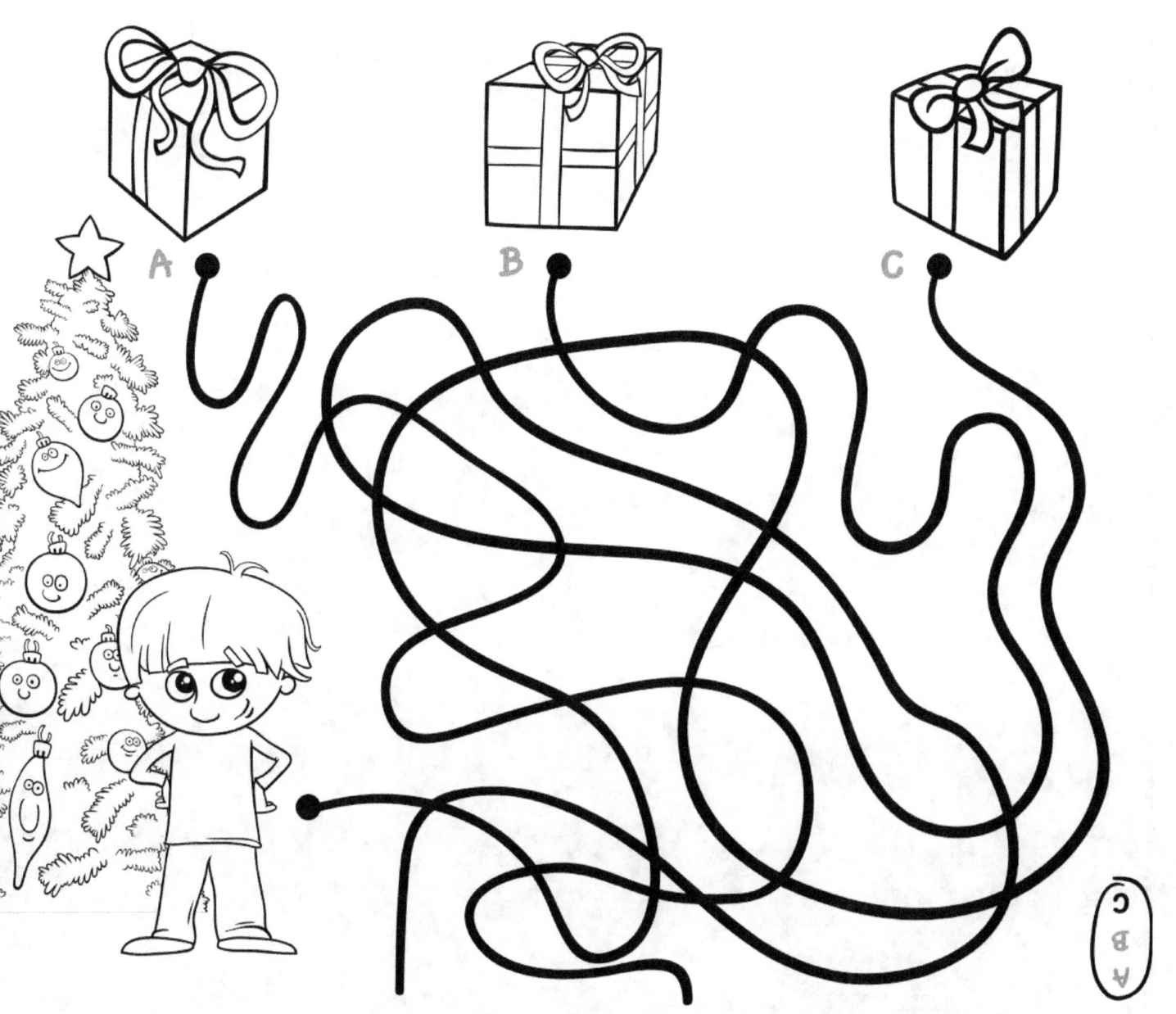

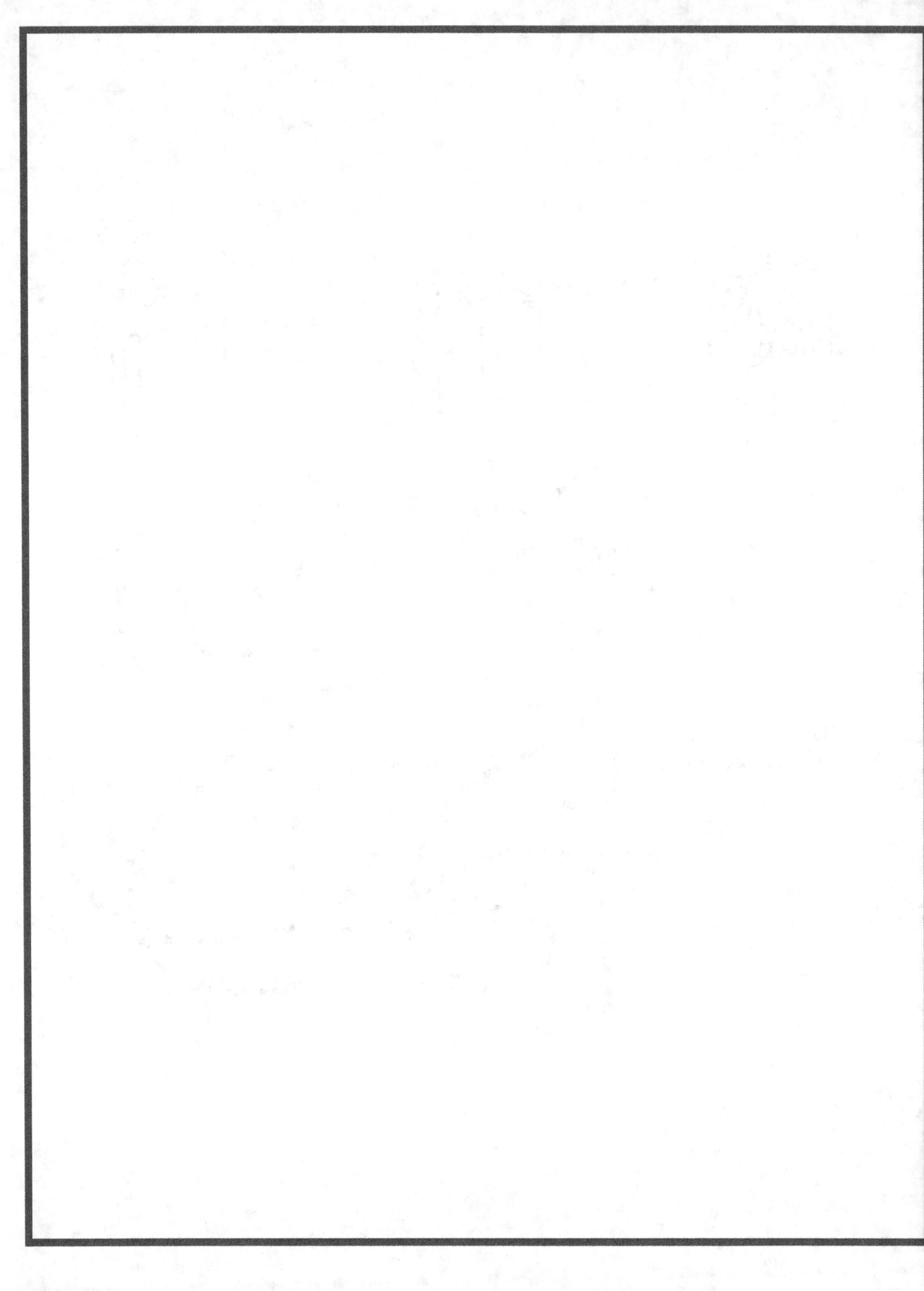

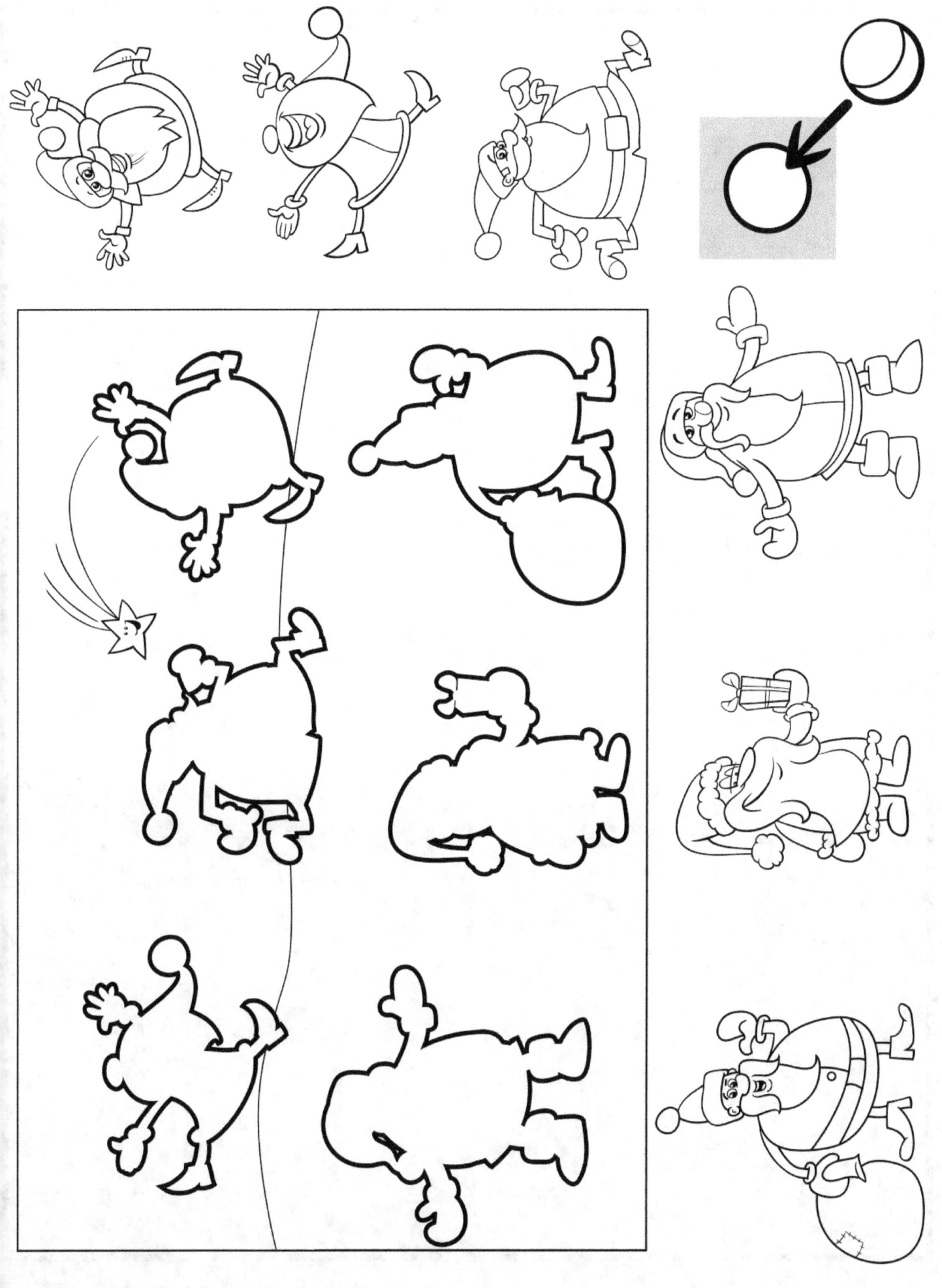

WHAT COMES NEXT?

1

2

3

4

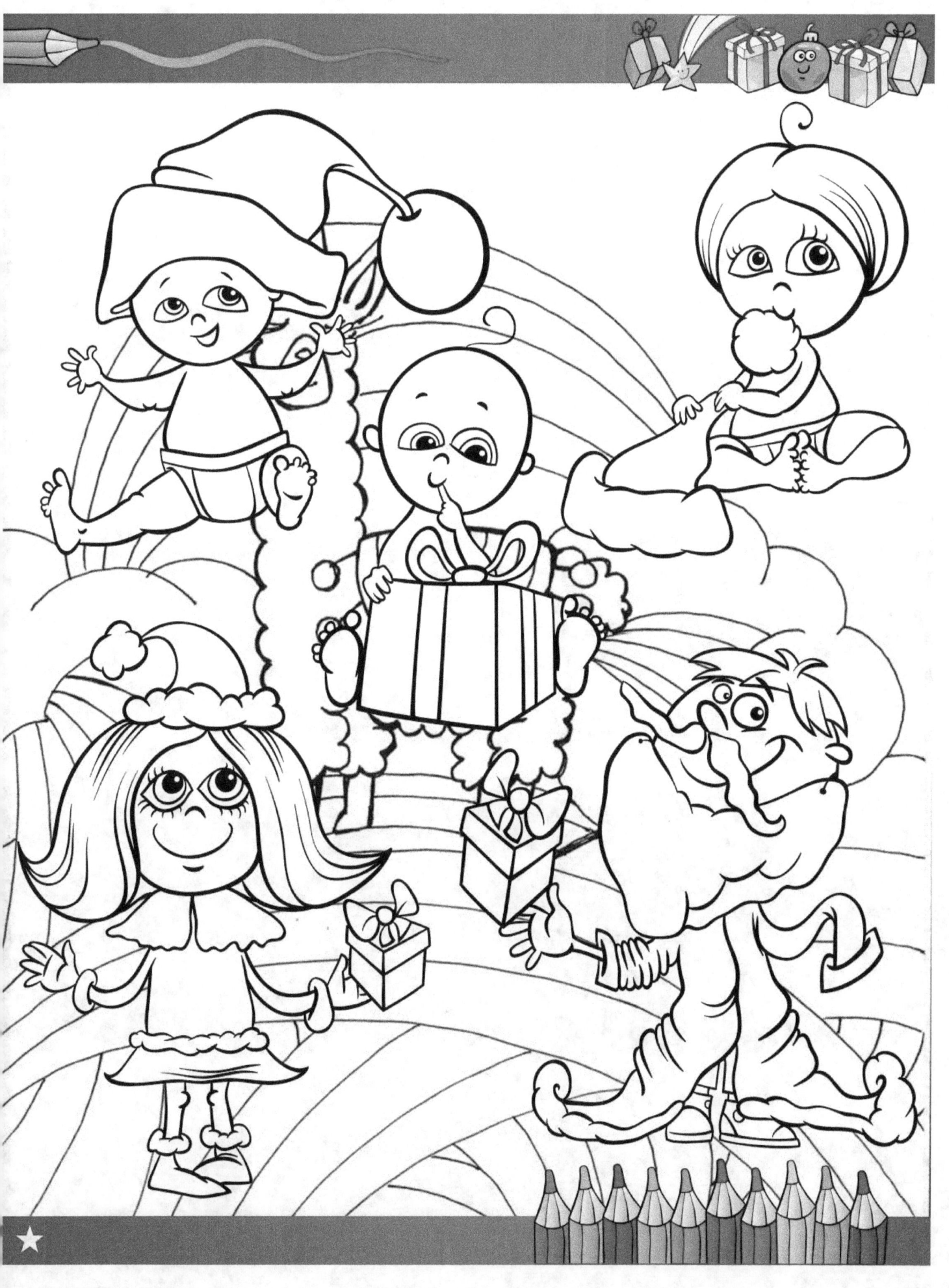

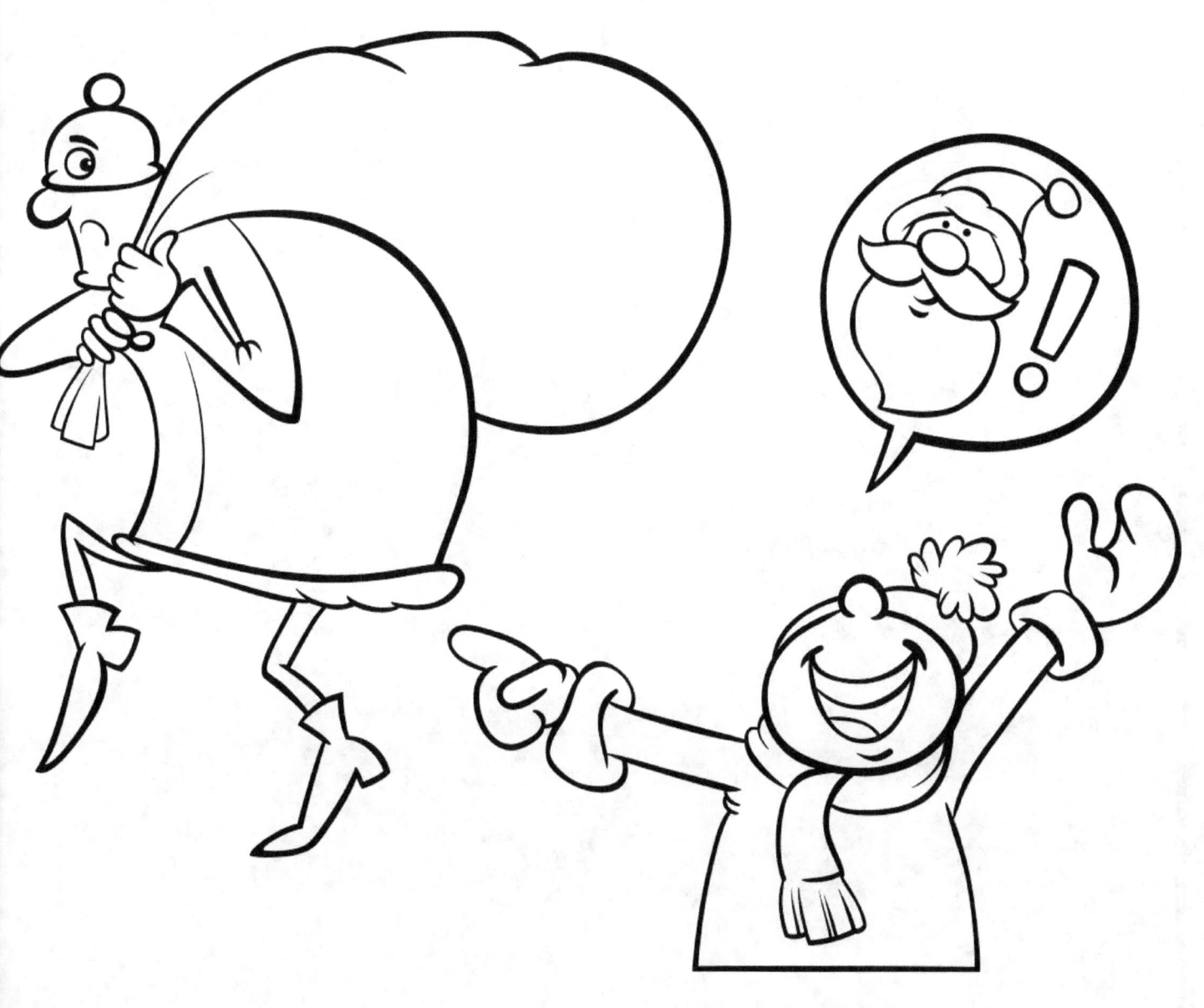

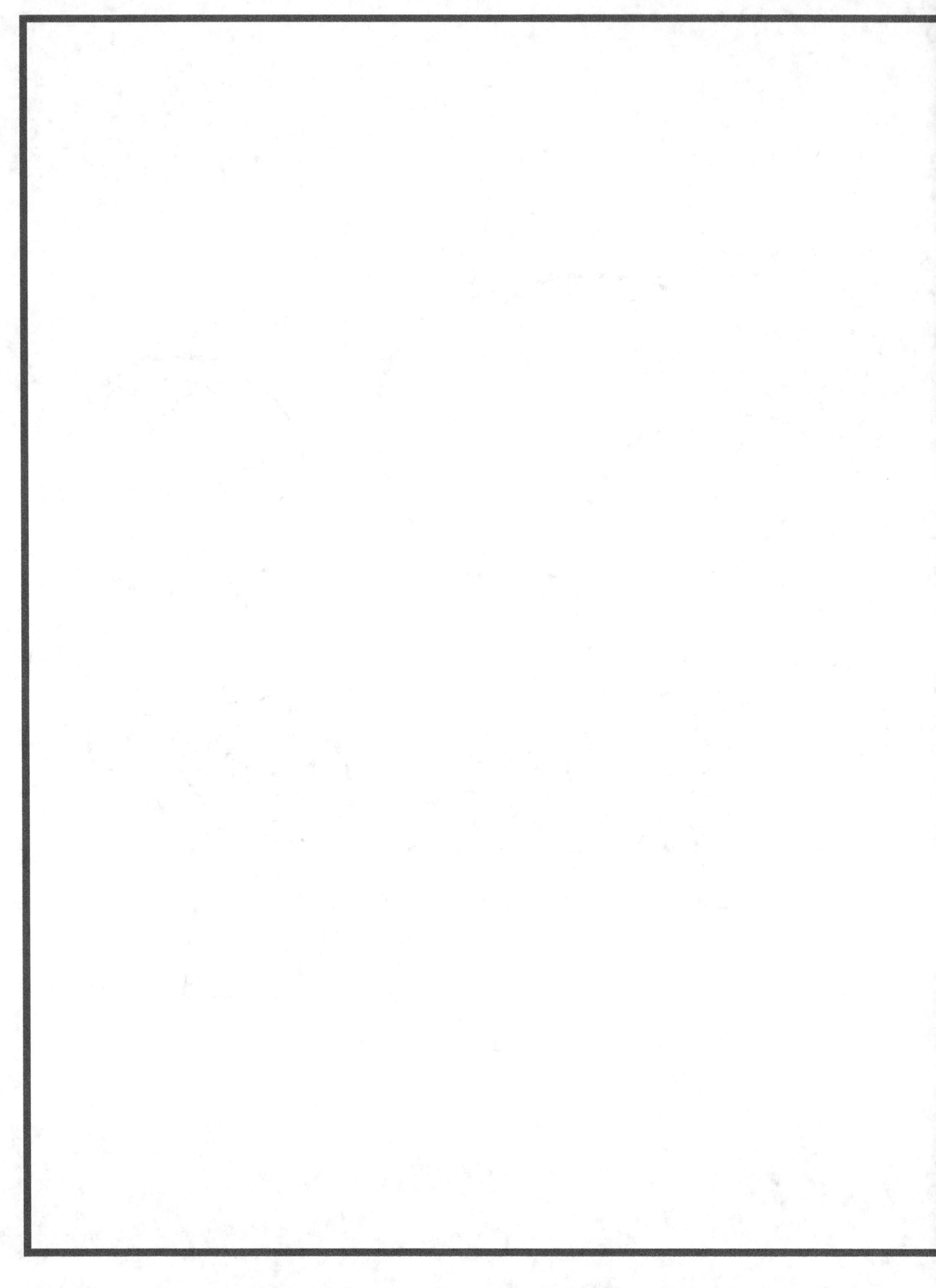

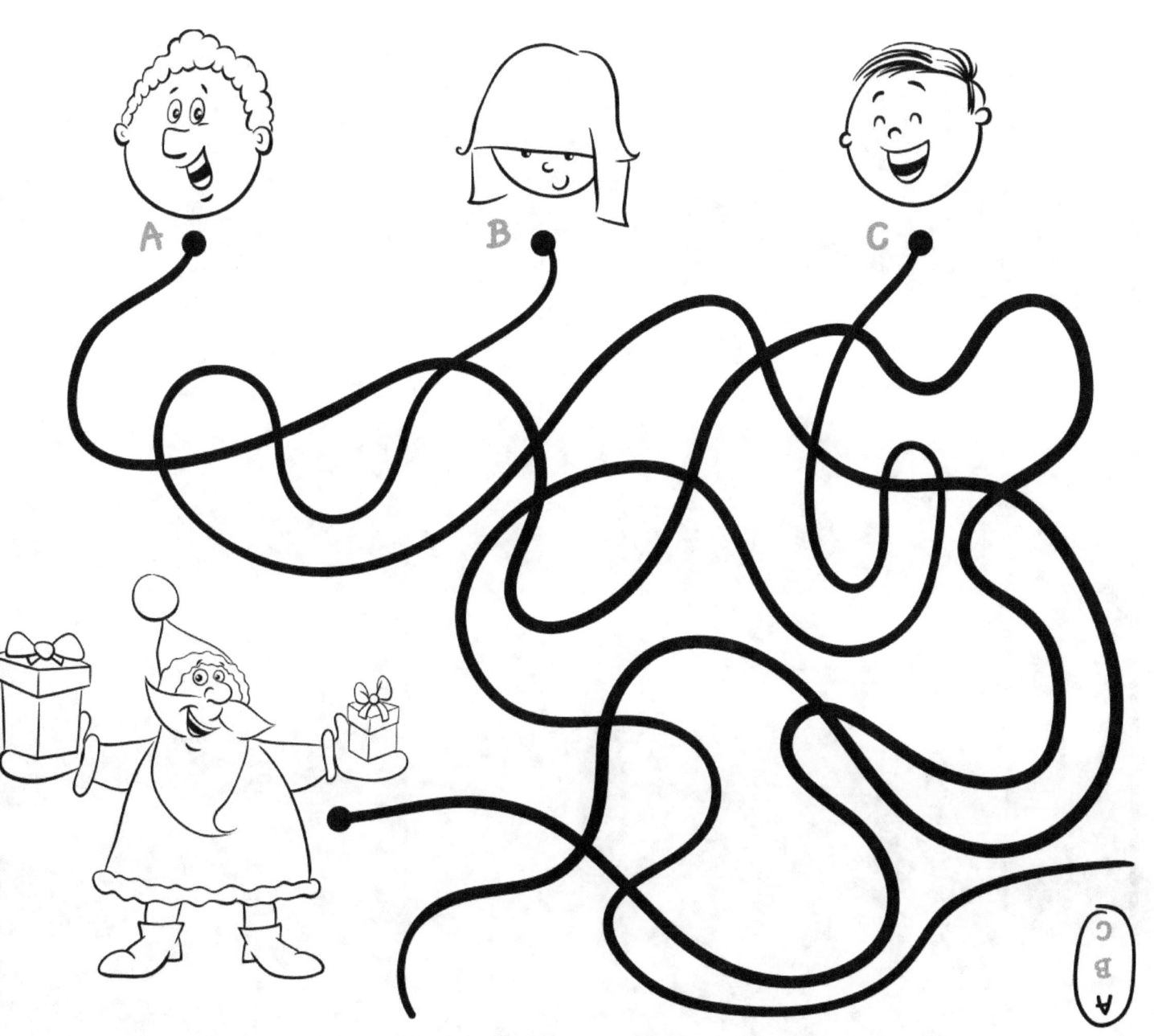

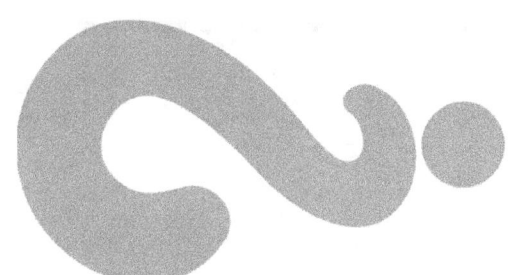

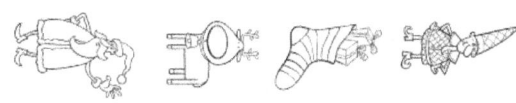

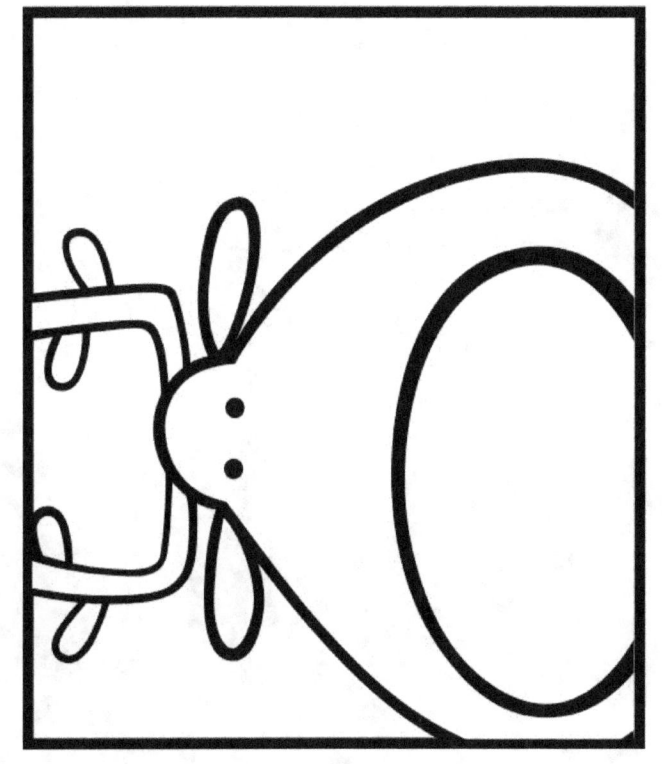

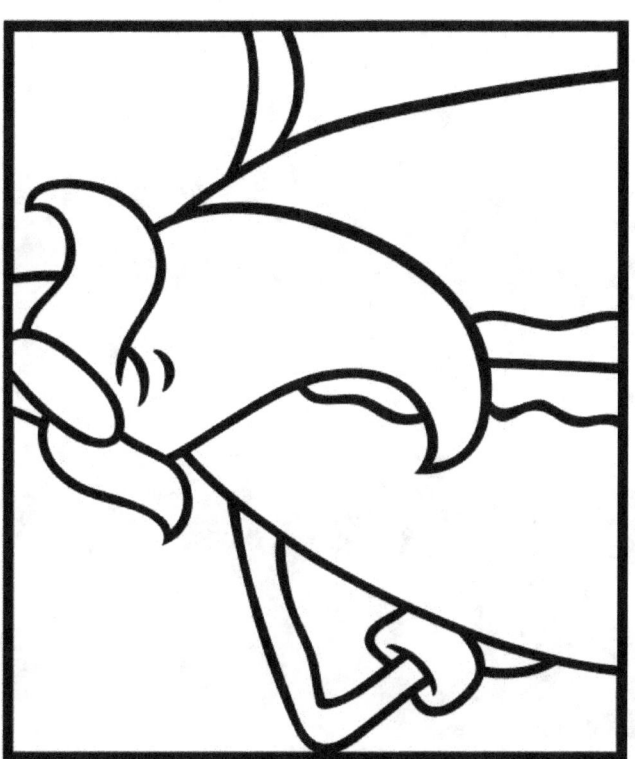

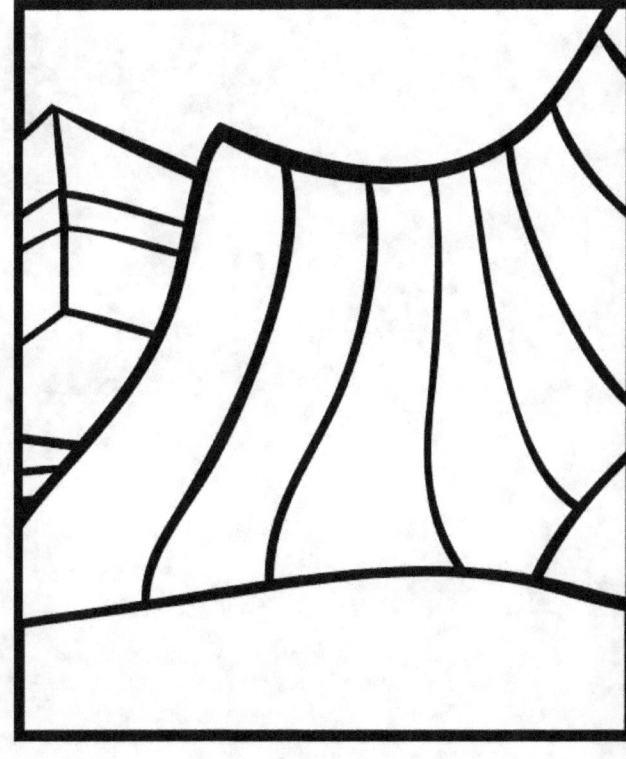

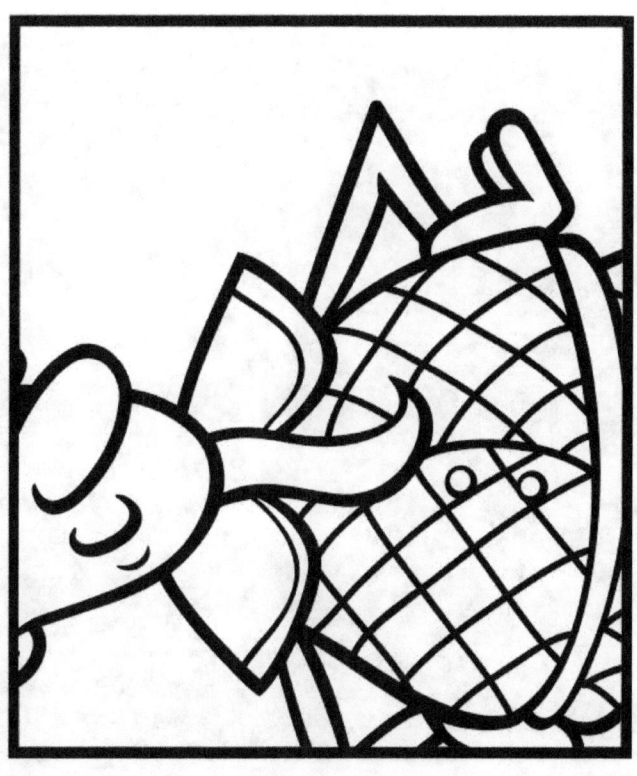

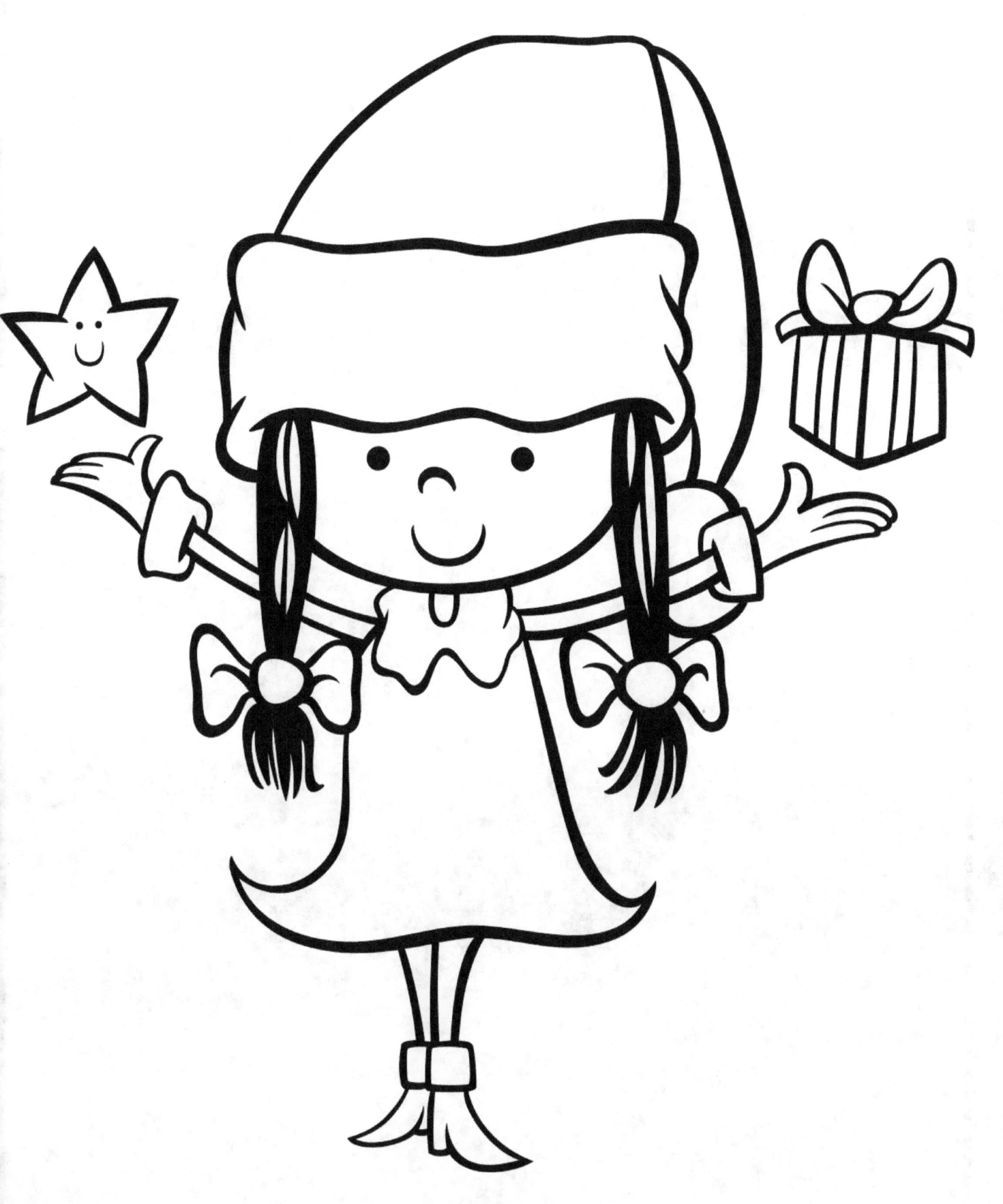

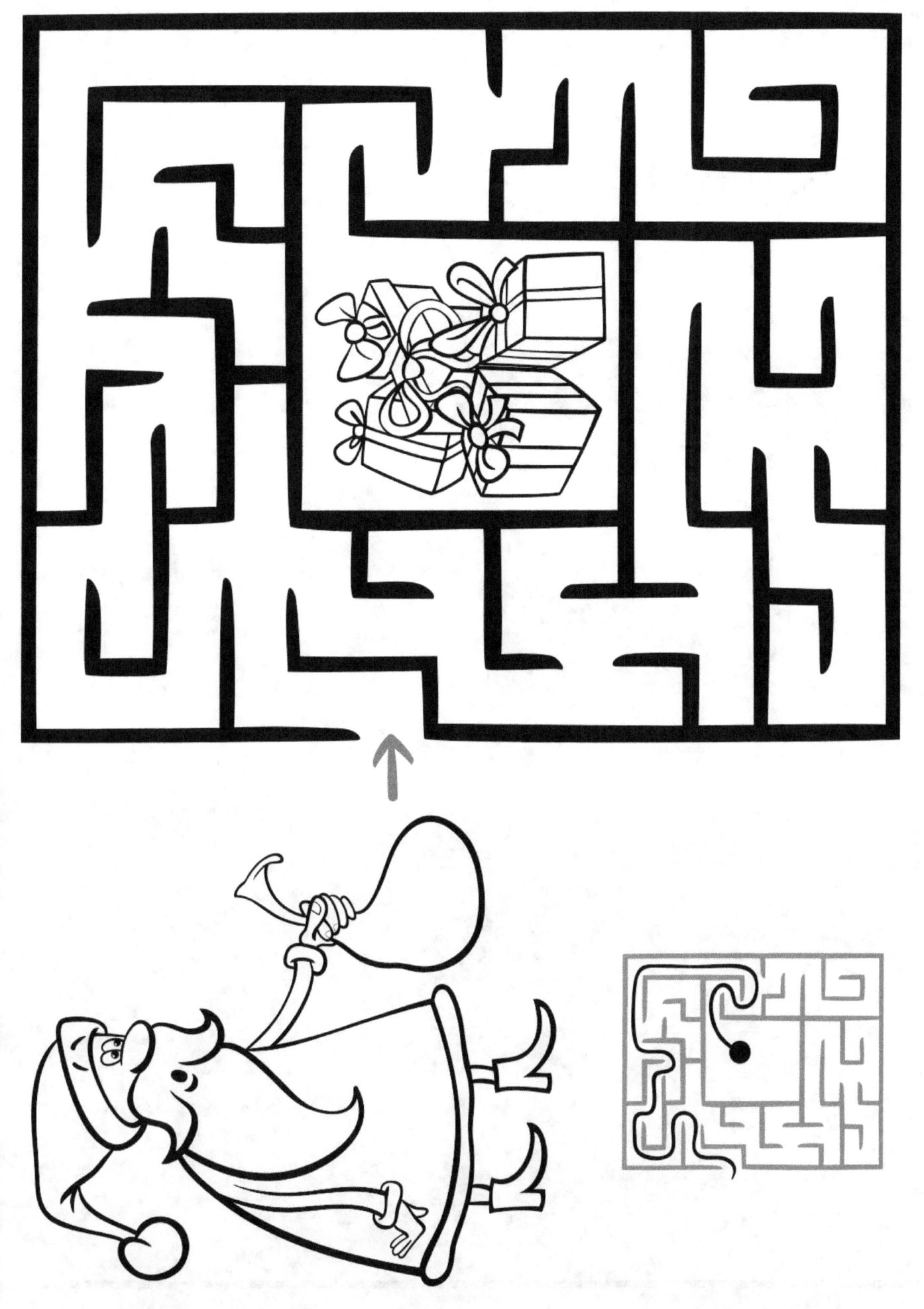

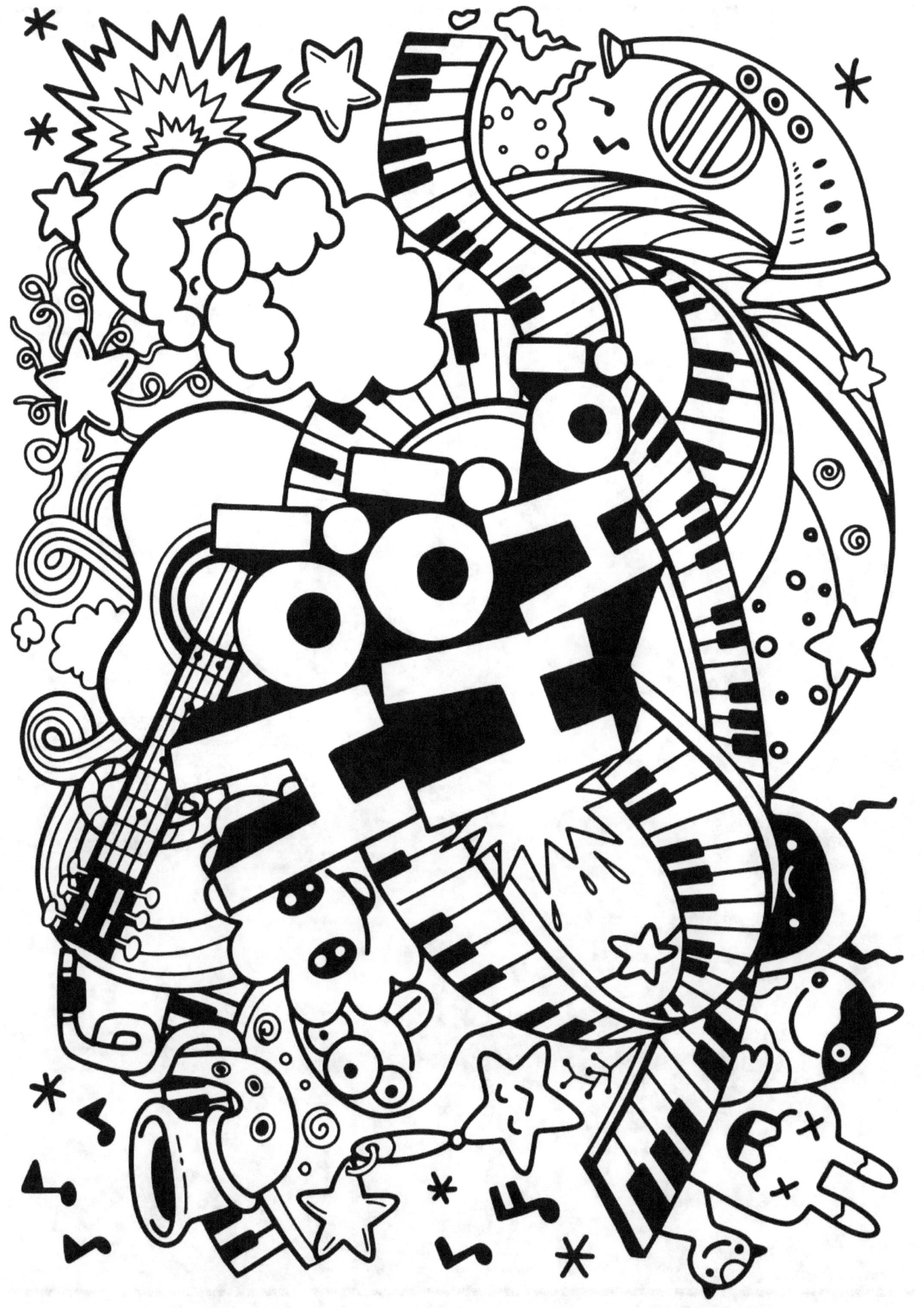

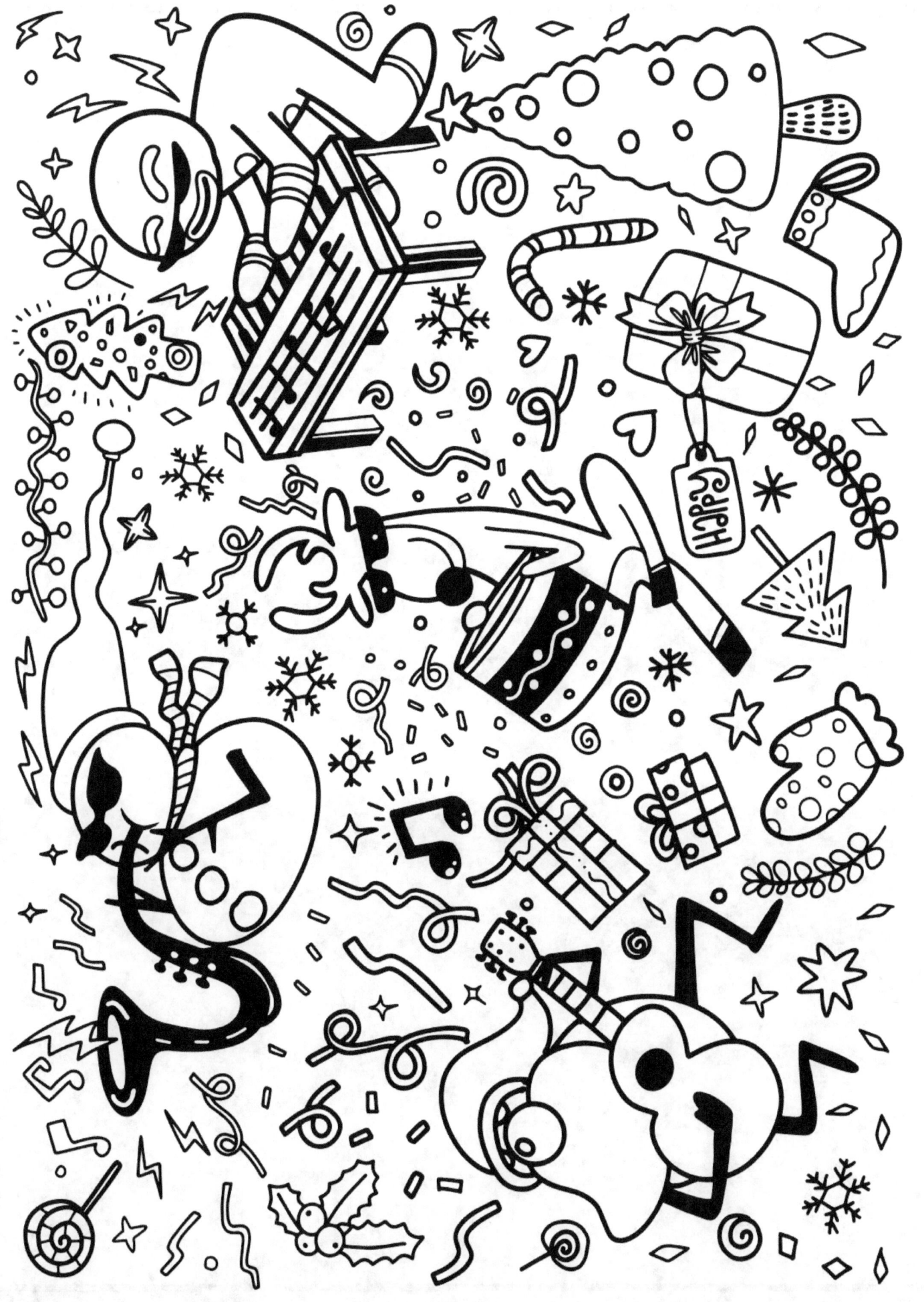

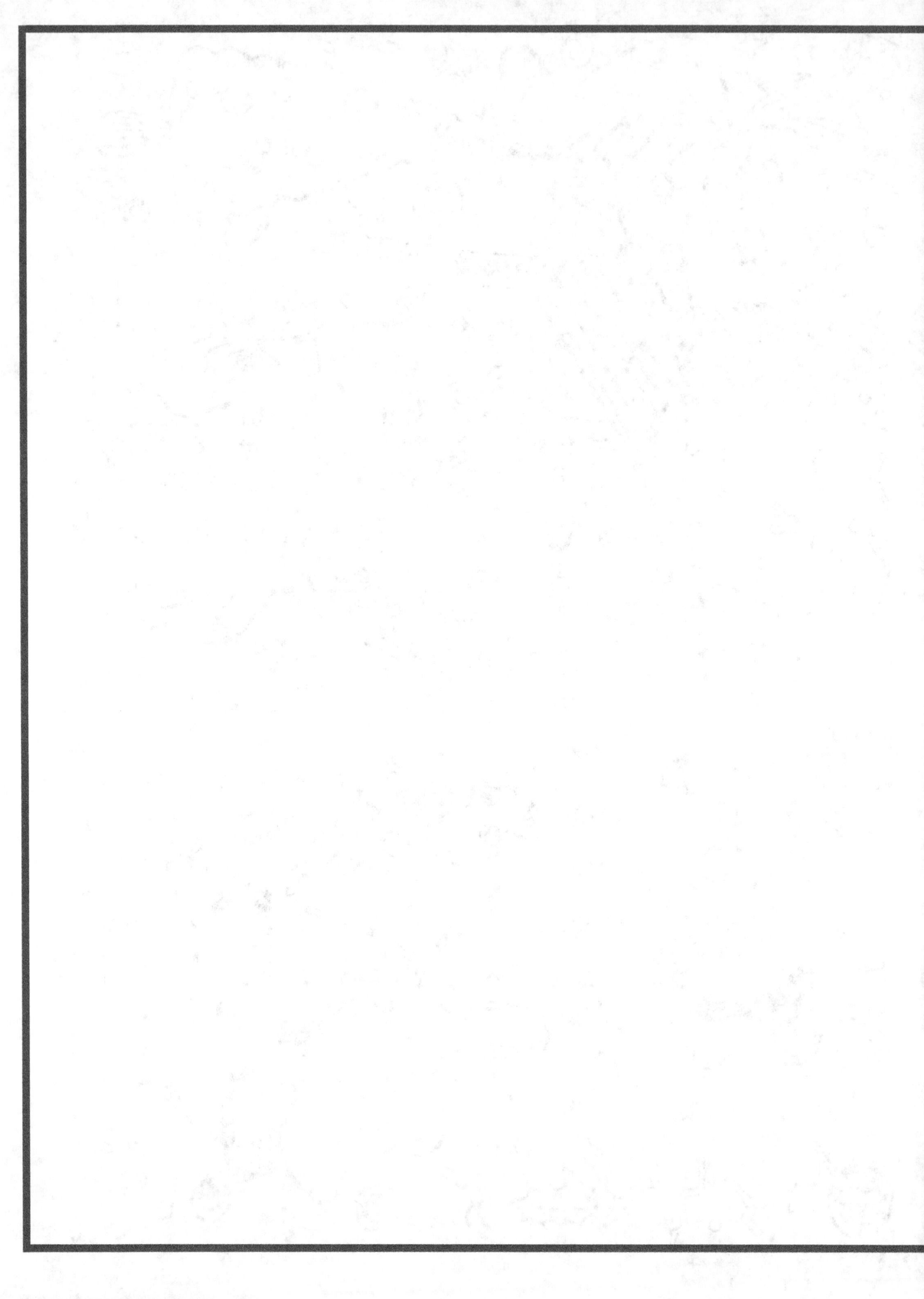

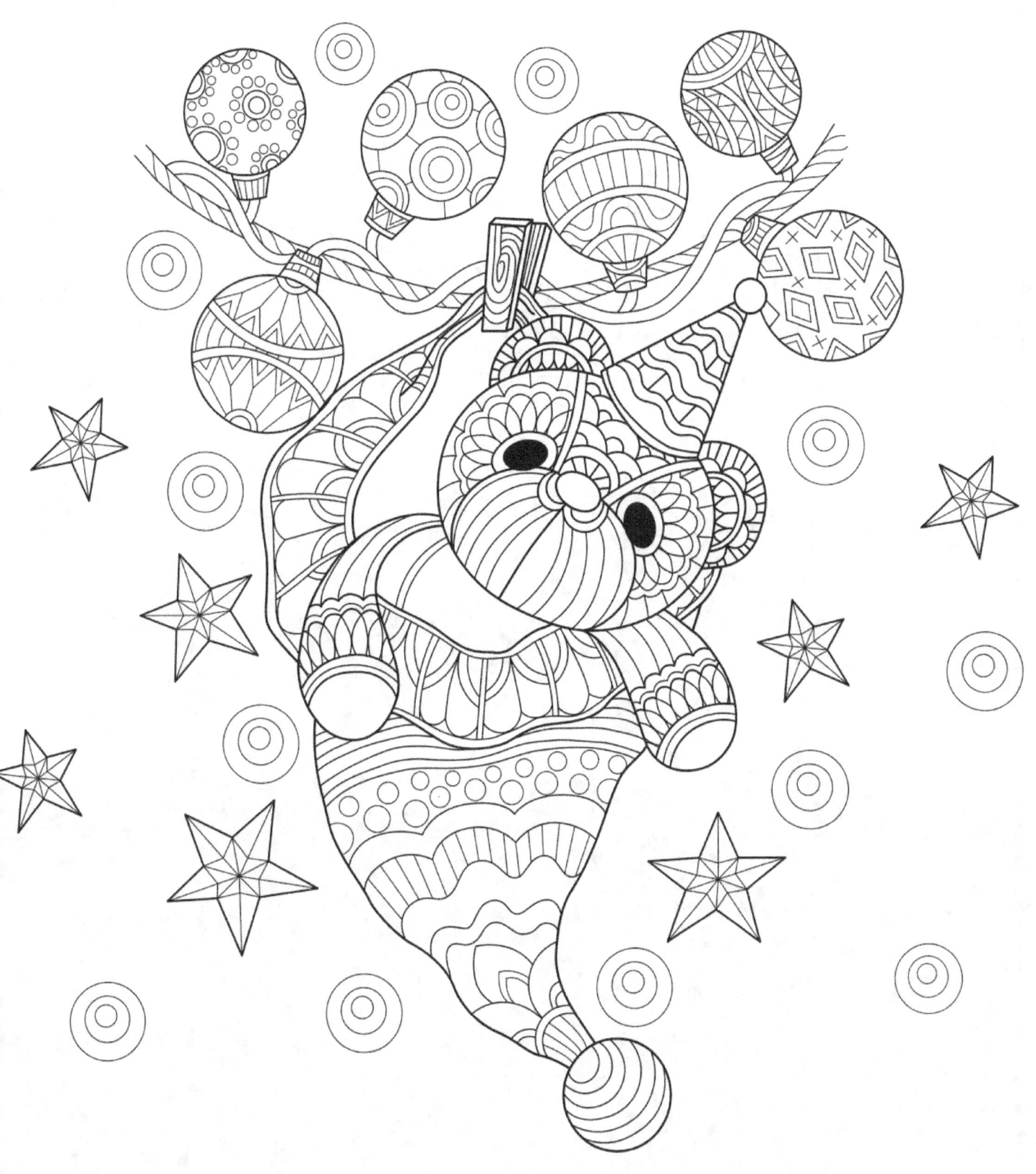

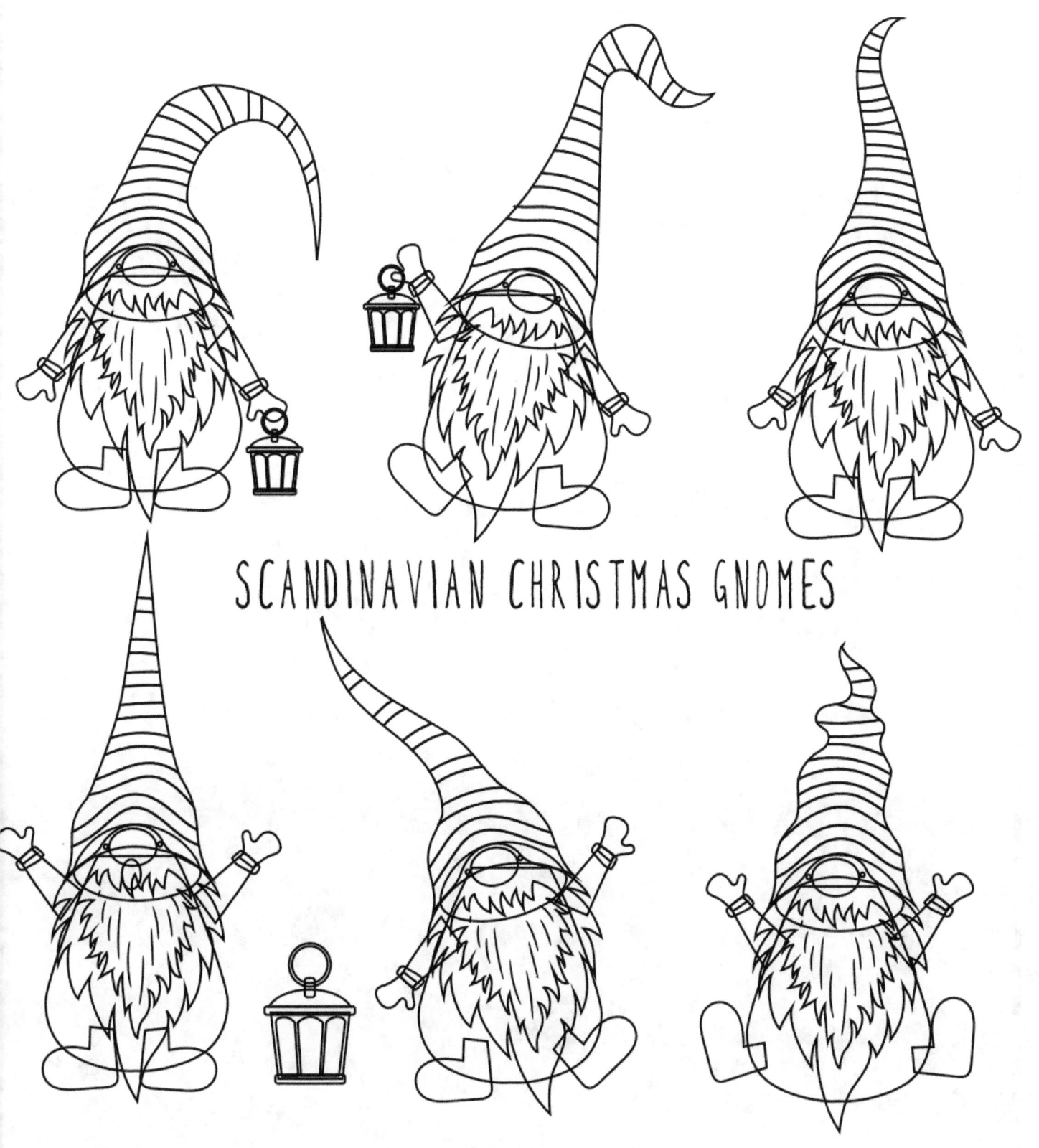

SCANDINAVIAN CHRISTMAS GNOMES

www.ingramcontent.com/pod-product-compliance
Lightning Source LLC
Chambersburg PA
CBHW081546220526
45467CB00010B/3343